I0490717

THE INKED CHRONICLES

A Journey Through the History and Meaning of Tattoos

RHYAN SCORPIO-RHYS

Copyright © 2023 by Rhyan Scorpio-Rhys

All rights reserved.

No part of this book may be reproduced in any form or by any electronic or mechanical means, including information storage and retrieval systems, without written permission from the author, except for the use of brief quotations in a book review.

CONTENTS

INTRODUCTION

Tattoos have been an integral part of human culture and self-expression for thousands of years. From the earliest marks etched onto the skin of our ancestors to the intricate, symbolic designs adorning the bodies of millions today, tattoos have served as personal statements, records of significant life events, and symbols of affiliation or belief. "The Inked Chronicles: A Journey Through the History and Meaning of Tattoos" aims to explore the fascinating world of tattoos by delving into their rich history, examining the meaning behind various designs, and tracing the evolution of tattooing as both an art form and a social phenomenon.

The purpose of this book is to provide a comprehensive and engaging overview of the world of tattoos, examining the various cultural, historical, and personal contexts that have shaped the practice over time. We will travel through the ages, from prehistoric cultures to ancient civilizations, exploring the role tattoos played in those societies and the meanings they held. We will also delve into the unique tattoo traditions of various tribes, religions, and military forces, highlighting the significance of tattoos as symbols of identity, spirituality, and loyalty.

As we move through history, we will examine the artistry and techniques behind tattoos, celebrating the pioneering artists who transformed the practice into the diverse and vibrant art form we know today. We will explore the symbolism and meaning of popular tattoo designs, from animals and flowers to mythological figures and geometric patterns, shedding light on the stories and beliefs they represent. Additionally, we will discuss the shifting social perceptions and taboos surrounding tattoos, as well as the importance of proper aftercare and health considerations.

Finally, we will look to the future of tattoos, considering the impact of technological advancements and the continued evolution of tattoo culture. As we embark on this journey, it is our hope that readers will gain a deeper appreciation for the art of tattooing, the history that has shaped it, and the personal and cultural significance it holds for countless individuals around the world.

Welcome to "The Inked Chronicles." Prepare to be inspired, enlightened, and forever changed by the indelible world of tattoos.

THE ANCIENT WORLD

In this chapter, we will journey back in time to the earliest origins of tattooing, exploring how ancient civilizations used tattoos for various purposes and examining the meanings behind their designs.

Prehistoric Tattoos

The history of tattoos can be traced back to the prehistoric era, as evidenced by the discovery of tattooed mummies and ancient tools that were likely used for tattooing. Ötzi the Iceman, a well-preserved mummy dating back to around 3300 BCE, was found in the Ötztal Alps with over 60 simple tattoos on his body. These tattoos, which consist of dots and lines, were likely created by rubbing charcoal into small incisions in the skin. While the exact purpose of Ötzi's tattoos remains unclear, some researchers believe that they may have been intended for therapeutic or medicinal purposes, as many of them are located on or near traditional acupuncture points.

Egyptian and Nubian Tattoos

The practice of tattooing was also present in ancient Egyptian and Nubian cultures, dating back to at least 2000 BCE. Mummies discovered in Egypt and Sudan have been found with tattoos, often consisting of geometric patterns, dots, and lines. Many of these tattoos were found on female mummies and are thought to have been symbols of fertility, protection during childbirth, or markers of social status. The ancient Egyptians also used tattoos for religious purposes, with some designs depicting deities such as Bes, the protector of households and childbirth.

Ancient Greek and Roman Tattoos

In ancient Greek and Roman societies, tattoos were used to mark criminals, slaves, and prisoners of war as a form of punishment and humiliation. The Greeks referred to tattoos as "stigmata," while the Romans called them "insigne stigmata." Despite this negative association, tattoos were also used by some Greek and Roman soldiers as symbols of bravery or to identify their military unit. Moreover, some ancient Greek writers, such as Herodotus, mentioned the tattooing practices of foreign cultures like the Scythians and Thracians, who used tattoos as markers of status and tribal affiliation.

Ancient Asian Tattoos

Tattooing was also practiced in ancient Asian cultures, with evidence of tattoos dating back to the Neolithic period in China, Japan, and Korea. In ancient China, tattoos were often used as a form of punishment, with criminals receiving facial tattoos to mark their transgressions. However, tattoos were also used for spiritual and decorative purposes, particularly among minority ethnic groups such as the Dulong and Dai people.

In Japan, the practice of tattooing, known as "irezumi," has a long and complex history. Early Japanese tattoos were often used to mark social status, with members of certain classes and professions, such as courtesans and firefighters, receiving tattoos to signify their roles. Over time, Japanese tattooing evolved into a highly intricate and artistic practice, with the creation of the full-body "horimono" tattoos that are still popular today.

In ancient Korea, tattoos were similarly used to mark social status or as a form of punishment. The Goguryeo, Baekje, and Silla kingdoms all practiced tattooing, with some evidence suggesting that tattoos were used to indicate rank among warriors or to denote membership in certain religious or spiritual groups.

As we have seen in this chapter, the ancient world was home to a wide variety of tattooing practices, each with its own unique cultural significance and meaning. In the following chapters, we will delve further into the history of tattoos, exploring the unique tattoo traditions of tribal societies, religious and spiritual communities, and military forces across the globe.

TRIBAL TATTOOS

I n this chapter, we will delve into the fascinating world of tribal tattoos, exploring their rich history and cultural significance in various indigenous societies. These tattoos often hold deep meanings and symbolism, reflecting the beliefs, traditions, and social structures of the tribes in which they originated.

Polynesian and Maori Tattoos

Polynesian tattoos, known as "tatau," have a rich history dating back over 2,000 years. These tattoos are characterized by their intricate, geometric patterns and are deeply ingrained in the culture and traditions of Polynesian people. Each Polynesian island group has its own unique tattoo styles and techniques, with designs varying between Samoa, Tonga, Tahiti, Hawaii, and New Zealand.

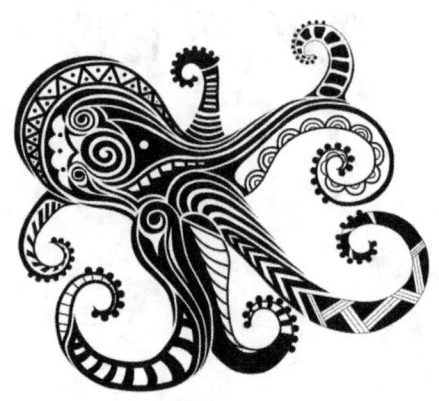

In New Zealand, the indigenous Maori people have a distinct tattooing tradition known as "ta moko." Ta moko tattoos are characterized by their bold, curvilinear patterns and the use of chisels to carve the design into the skin, leaving raised scars. These tattoos serve as markers of social status, with specific designs denoting rank, ancestry, and personal achievements. The facial moko, or "moko kauae" for women and "moko rangatira" for men, is particularly significant, as it represents a person's identity and lineage.

Native American Tattoos

Tattooing was practiced among many Native American tribes, with designs often reflecting the natural world, spiritual beliefs, and tribal affiliations. Some tribes used tattoos as rites of passage, while others marked warriors with tattoos symbolizing their prowess in battle. Methods of tattooing varied among tribes, with some using sharpened bone, shells, or cactus needles to puncture the skin and apply pigments made from natural materials such as soot, crushed minerals, or plant dyes.

Some notable Native American tattoo traditions include the Inuit, who used tattoos to symbolize hunting achievements and spiritual protection, and the Iroquois, who used tattoos as markers of clan affiliation and social status. The Pueblo people, meanwhile, tattooed women's hands and wrists to signify their skill in pottery making.

African Tribal Tattoos

African tribal tattoos vary greatly in design and symbolism, reflecting the diverse cultural traditions found across the continent. Some tribes used tattoos as a form of body art, while others employed them for spiritual, medicinal, or social purposes. The Berber people of North Africa, for instance, used tattoos to symbolize fertility, protection, and cultural identity. In West Africa, the Yoruba and Fon people used tattoos known as "sacred markings" or "scarification" for spiritual purposes, with designs believed to invoke divine protection and guidance.

In Central Africa, the Mursi and Surma tribes of Ethiopia and South Sudan practice lip plate tattooing, in which a young woman's lower lip is pierced and gradually stretched to accommodate a large, decorative clay plate. This tradition is believed to signify beauty and maturity, as well as deter potential kidnappers or slavers.

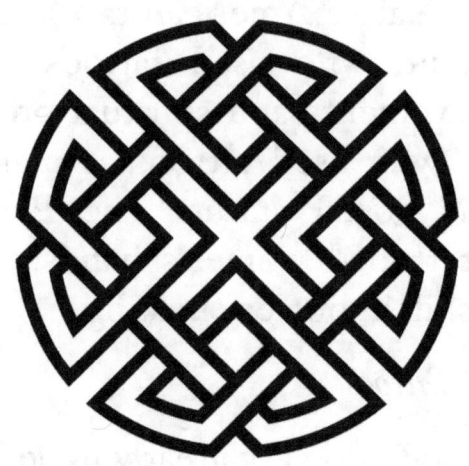

Celtic and Viking Tattoos

Celtic tattoos are characterized by their intricate, interlacing patterns and knotwork designs, which often feature symbols such as animals, crosses, or the iconic "triquetra" (three-cornered) motif. While concrete evidence of ancient Celtic tattooing is scarce, some historians believe that the Celts likely practiced tattooing as a form of body art or to denote tribal affiliation.

Viking tattoos are similarly shrouded in mystery, with little direct evidence of their existence in the historical record. However, some scholars believe that the Vikings may have used tattoos for various purposes, such as marking warriors, commemorating battles, or displaying symbols of Norse mythology and religious beliefs. Designs may have included Norse runes, depictions of gods like Odin or Thor, and symbols such as the Valknut or the Vegvísir. Some accounts from Arab travelers who encountered Vikings during the 9th and 10th centuries mention their tattooed bodies, suggesting that tattooing may have been a part of Viking culture.

In this chapter, we have explored the rich and diverse world of tribal tattoos, delving into the unique tattooing traditions of various indigenous societies across the globe. These tattoos often hold deep cultural significance, reflecting the beliefs, traditions, and social structures of the tribes in which they originated. As we continue our journey through the history and meaning of tattoos, we will examine the role of tattoos in religious and spiritual practices, highlighting the ways in which people have used tattoos to express their faith and connect with the divine.

TATTOOS IN RELIGION AND SPIRITUALITY

Throughout history, tattoos have held deep religious and spiritual significance in various cultures and belief systems. In this chapter, we will explore the role of tattoos in religious and spiritual practices, examining their symbolism and the ways in which they have been used to express devotion, protection, and connection with the divine.

Christian Tattoos

Christian tattoos have a long and storied history, with some of the earliest examples dating back to the Coptic Christians of Egypt in the 4th century. These early Christian tattoos often featured religious symbols such as crosses, doves, and icons of saints, serving as markers of faith and devotion. Pilgrimage tattoos were also popular among medieval Christians, who would travel to sacred sites such as Jerusalem and Bethlehem and receive tattoos to commemorate their spiritual journey.

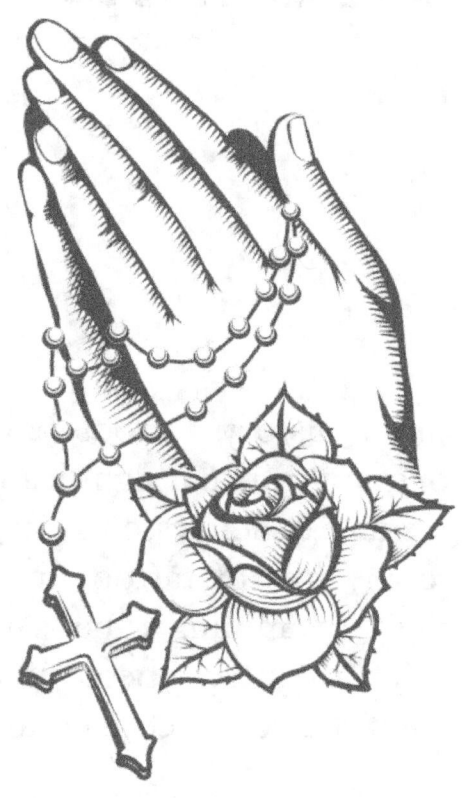

In modern times, Christian tattoos continue to be popular, with designs ranging from traditional symbols like crosses and angels to more contemporary interpretations, such as Bible verses, portraits of Jesus, and religious scenes.

Buddhist Tattoos

In Buddhist tradition, tattoos have long been used for spiritual and protective purposes. The Sak Yant, or "sacred tattoo," is a form of tattooing practiced in Thailand, Cambodia, and Laos. These tattoos, which are believed to impart mystical powers and protection, often feature sacred Buddhist symbols, geometric designs, and Pali script. The Sak Yant tattoos are traditionally administered by Buddhist monks or specialized tattoo masters known as "ajarns," who perform a ritual blessing during the tattooing process.

Another example of Buddhist tattooing can be found in Japan, where certain sects of Buddhism, such as the Shingon and Tendai schools, have been known to use tattoos to represent religious devotion and spiritual attainment.

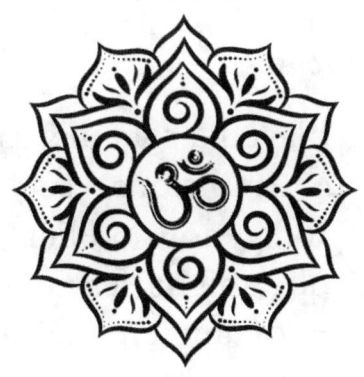

Hindu Tattoos

Hindu tattoos are characterized by their rich symbolism and intricate designs, which often draw from the religion's vast pantheon of gods, sacred symbols, and sacred texts. Popular Hindu tattoo designs include the Om symbol, which represents the sacred sound and vibration of the universe; the lotus flower, a symbol of purity and spiritual awakening; and depictions of various deities, such as Ganesha, the elephant-headed god of wisdom and new beginnings.

Henna, a temporary form of body art, is also deeply rooted in Hindu culture and tradition. Henna tattoos, known as "mehndi," are often applied to the hands and feet of women during special occasions, such as weddings and religious festivals. Mehndi designs are typically intricate and elaborate, featuring floral patterns and symbolic motifs that are believed to bring good luck and protection.

Other Spiritual Tattoos

Tattoos have also played a role in various other spiritual and religious traditions, such as paganism, shamanism, and indigenous belief systems. Pagan tattoos, for example, might feature symbols of nature, the elements, or ancient deities from various mythologies. Shamanic tattoos, on the other hand, may incorporate symbols of animal spirits, sacred plants, or other elements of the shamanic worldview.

In indigenous cultures, spiritual tattoos may serve as markers of rites of passage, symbols of protection, or connections to ancestral spirits. For example, the indigenous Ainu people of Japan have a tattooing tradition known as "ainu irezumi," which involves tattooing intricate designs around the mouths of women to ward off evil spirits and ensure a safe passage to the afterlife.

In this chapter, we have explored the profound religious and spiritual significance of tattoos in various cultures and belief systems. As we continue our journey through the history and meaning of tattoos, we will examine the role of tattoos in military traditions, highlighting the ways in which soldiers have used tattoos to symbolize their allegiance, commemorate their service, and honor fallen comrades. From ancient warriors to modern-day military personnel, the use of tattoos in military traditions serves as a powerful reminder of the bravery, sacrifice, and camaraderie that define the experiences of those who serve.

As we delve into this fascinating aspect of tattoo culture, we gain a deeper understanding of the complex emotions and narratives that tattoos can convey, further reinforcing their status as a unique and powerful form of self-expression and storytelling.

TATTOOS IN MILITARY TRADITIONS

Tattoos have long played a significant role in military traditions across the globe. In this chapter, we will explore the history and meaning of military tattoos, examining how they have been used to symbolize allegiance, camaraderie, and personal achievements in various armed forces throughout time.

Ancient Military Tattoos

Evidence of tattoos in ancient military forces can be found in various civilizations, from the Greeks and Romans to the Scythians and Thracians. As mentioned in Chapter 1, some Greek and Roman soldiers used tattoos as symbols of bravery or to identify their military unit. Similarly, the Scythians and Thracians used tattoos to mark their warriors with symbols of their tribe and military accomplishments.

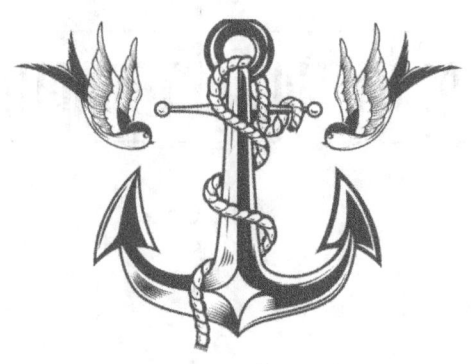

Naval Tattoos

Naval tattoos have a long and storied history, dating back to the 18th century when European sailors began exploring the Pacific and encountering Polynesian tattooing traditions. Many sailors adopted tattoos as a way to commemorate their travels, mark their rank, or signify specific achievements and experiences.

Popular naval tattoo designs include anchors, which symbolize stability and a sailor's connection to the sea; swallows, which were believed to ensure a safe return home; and fully-rigged ships, which represented a sailor's journey around Cape Horn, one of the most treacherous maritime routes.

Modern Military Tattoos

In modern military forces, tattoos continue to be popular as a means of expressing solidarity, commemorating service, and honoring fallen comrades. Many soldiers choose to get tattoos that represent their branch of service, such as the eagle, globe, and anchor emblem of the United States Marine Corps or the crossed rifles of the United States Army infantry.

Other popular military tattoo designs include the "death's head" or skull, which symbolizes the acceptance of one's mortality and the dangers of combat; dog tags, which represent a soldier's identification and commitment to their comrades; and memorial tattoos, which often feature the names or portraits of fallen friends and loved ones.

In some cases, military tattoos may also be used to signify membership in specific units or elite forces, such as the Special Forces, Navy SEALs, or Army Rangers. These tattoos often feature specialized insignia or symbols unique to the particular group.

Tattoos and Military Regulations

While tattoos have a long history in military culture, they have also been subject to various regulations and restrictions depending on the specific armed force and time period. In recent years, many military organizations have updated their tattoo policies to accommodate the growing popularity of tattoos in the general population. However, some restrictions still apply, such as limitations on the size, location, and content of tattoos, to ensure that they do not interfere with a soldier's appearance or performance.

In this chapter, we have explored the rich history and meaning of military tattoos, highlighting the ways in which they have been used to symbolize allegiance, camaraderie, and personal achievements in various armed forces throughout time. As we continue our journey through the history and meaning of tattoos, we will examine the evolution of tattooing as an art form and the societal perceptions of tattoos in different cultures and historical periods.

THE EVOLUTION OF TATTOOING AS AN ART FORM AND SOCIETAL PERCEPTIONS

I n this chapter, we will explore the evolution of tattooing as an art form, tracing its development from ancient practices to the modern tattoo industry. We will also examine the shifting societal perceptions of tattoos, highlighting the various factors that have influenced their acceptance and stigma throughout history.

From Traditional Techniques to Modern Innovations

The art of tattooing has come a long way from its ancient origins, with significant advancements in both technique and technology. Traditional tattooing methods, such as hand-tapping, stick and poke, and chiseling, are still practiced in some cultures and have experienced a resurgence in popularity as part of the modern "tribal" tattoo movement.

The invention of the electric tattoo machine in the late 19th century revolutionized the tattoo industry, allowing for greater precision, speed, and variety in tattoo designs. Modern tattoo machines use an electromagnetic coil system to rapidly move the tattoo needle in and out of the skin, depositing ink with each puncture.

Today's tattoo artists have access to a wide range of tools, inks, and styles, allowing them to create intricate, detailed, and colorful designs that were previously unimaginable. The rise of social media and online platforms has also contributed to the growth and diversification of tattoo art, as artists can easily share their work and connect with clients and fellow artists from around the world.

Societal Perceptions of Tattoos: Stigma and Acceptance

The societal perception of tattoos has fluctuated greatly over time, influenced by factors such as culture, religion, and social class. In some societies, tattoos have been embraced as symbols of status, identity, and spirituality, while in others, they have been stigmatized as marks of criminality, deviance, or immorality.

In the Western world, tattoos have historically been associated with marginalized groups, such as sailors, criminals, and circus performers. However, the 20th century saw a gradual shift in attitudes towards tattoos, with the rise of countercultural movements such as the Beat Generation, the Hippie movement, and Punk Rock, which embraced tattoos as expressions of rebellion and individuality.

In recent decades, tattoos have become increasingly mainstream, with people from all walks of life and social backgrounds choosing to get inked. A growing number of celebrities and public figures, from athletes to actors, proudly display their tattoos, further contributing to their normalization and acceptance.

Despite this growing acceptance, tattoos still carry a degree of stigma in some social and professional settings. Many workplaces have dress codes that require tattoos to be covered, and some individuals may still face discrimination or judgment based on their tattoos.

The Future of Tattooing

As tattooing continues to evolve as an art form and cultural practice, new trends and innovations are constantly emerging. Developments in tattoo technology, such as digital tattoo machines and advanced ink formulations, promise to further expand the possibilities of tattoo art.

In addition, the growing acceptance and visibility of tattoos in mainstream culture have opened up new opportunities for tattoo artists and enthusiasts alike. Tattoo conventions, art exhibitions, and educational programs are now commonplace, fostering a greater appreciation for the history, techniques, and cultural significance of tattooing.

In this chapter, we have explored the evolution of tattooing as an art form and the shifting societal perceptions of tattoos throughout history. As we conclude our journey through the history and meaning of tattoos, we can appreciate the diverse ways in which tattoos have served as expressions of identity, faith, and creativity across cultures and time periods.

THE SYMBOLISM AND MEANINGS OF TATTOOS

I n this chapter, we will explore the symbolism and meanings behind various types of tattoos, delving into the rich imagery and cultural significance that can be found in different tattoo designs. From animals and flowers to mythology and abstract art, tattoos can convey a wide range of messages and emotions, allowing individuals to express their unique identities and stories.

Animal Tattoos and Their Meanings

Animal tattoos are popular for their rich symbolism and the personal connections people may have with particular animals. Some common animal tattoo meanings include:

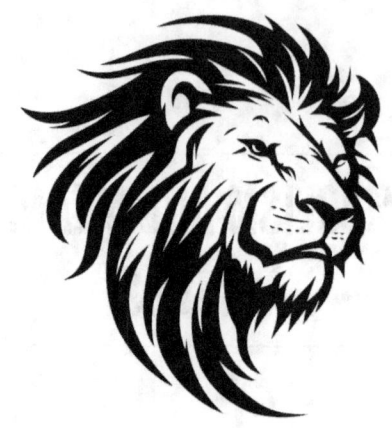

- Lion: The lion often symbolizes strength, courage, and leadership, reflecting its status as the "king of the jungle."
- Wolf: Wolves can represent loyalty, family, and the balance between the wild and the domestic, as they are known for their strong pack bonds and fierce independence.
- Elephant: Elephants are often associated with wisdom, patience, and memory, due to their long lifespans and complex social structures.
- Phoenix: The mythical phoenix symbolizes rebirth, transformation, and renewal, as it is said to rise from its own ashes to begin a new life cycle.
- Butterfly: Butterflies often represent transformation, growth, and beauty, reflecting the metamorphosis they undergo from caterpillar to winged adult.

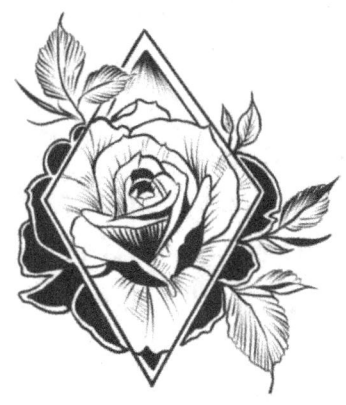

Floral Tattoos and Their Symbolism

Floral tattoos are popular for their aesthetic appeal and the diverse meanings associated with different flowers. Some examples of floral tattoo symbolism include:

- Rose: Roses often symbolize love, passion, and beauty, with different colors representing various aspects of love, such as red for romantic love and yellow for friendship.
- Lotus: The lotus flower is a symbol of purity, spiritual awakening, and enlightenment, as it grows from the muddy depths to blossom above the water's surface.
- Cherry blossom: In Japanese culture, cherry blossoms represent the fleeting nature of life and beauty, as they bloom for a short time before falling to the ground.

- Sunflower: Sunflowers symbolize warmth, happiness, and positivity, reflecting their vibrant color and the way they turn their faces towards the sun.
- Lily: Lilies are often associated with purity, innocence, and renewal, and are frequently used in religious and funerary contexts.

Mythological and Cultural Tattoos

Mythological and cultural tattoos draw from the rich stories and iconography of various belief systems and historical periods. Some examples include:

- Greek gods and goddesses: Tattoos of figures from Greek mythology can represent specific traits or virtues, such as wisdom (Athena), love (Aphrodite), or strength (Hercules).
- Norse mythology: Norse tattoos often feature runes, depictions of gods like Odin and Thor, and symbols such as the Valknut or Vegvísir.
- Egyptian symbols: Ancient Egyptian tattoos may include designs of the Eye of Horus (protection), the Ankh (eternal life), or the scarab beetle (transformation and rebirth).
- Celtic knotwork: Intricate Celtic knot designs can symbolize the

interconnectedness of life, the cycles of nature, or the eternal nature of love.

Text and Script Tattoos

Text and script tattoos allow individuals to express their thoughts, beliefs, or emotions through the power of the written word. Common examples include:

- Quotes: Inspirational or meaningful quotes from literature, poetry, or song lyrics.
- Names: The names of loved ones or important figures in the individual's life.
- Dates: Significant dates, such as birthdates or anniversaries, commemorating important life events.
- Symbols: Text-based symbols, such as the Chinese characters, Arabic calligraphy, or Sanskrit script, representing specific words, concepts, or virtues.

Abstract and Geometric Tattoos

Abstract and geometric tattoos often focus on the visual impact of shapes, patterns, and lines, rather than specific symbolic meanings. Examples include:

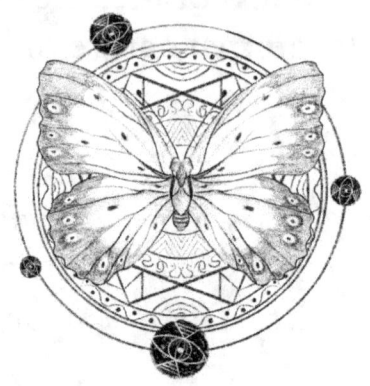

- Mandalas: Intricate, circular designs often used in Hinduism and Buddhism to represent the universe, spiritual growth, or meditation.
- Tribal patterns: Bold, black lines and shapes inspired by traditional tribal tattoo designs from cultures such as the Polynesians, Native Americans, or African tribes.
- Sacred geometry: Designs based on geometric shapes and patterns, such as the Flower of Life, Metatron's Cube, or the Sri Yantra, believed to hold spiritual or metaphysical significance.
- Minimalist designs: Simple, understated shapes and lines that convey meaning through their visual impact, such as a single triangle representing strength or a minimalist heart representing love.

In this chapter, we have explored the diverse symbolism and meanings behind various types of tattoos, shedding light on the rich cultural significance and personal connections that can be found in different tattoo designs. From animals and flowers to mythology and abstract art, tattoos offer a powerful medium for self-expression, allowing individuals to share their unique stories and identities through the language of ink.

TATTOO TABOOS AND SOCIAL PERCEPTIONS

I n this chapter, we will examine the various taboos and social perceptions surrounding tattoos, exploring how attitudes towards tattoos have shifted across different cultures and time periods. From legal restrictions to workplace policies, the stigma associated with tattoos has been influenced by a variety of factors, shaping the complex social landscape that surrounds tattoo art and culture.

The Stigma Surrounding Tattoos in Different Cultures and Time Periods

Throughout history, tattoos have been both revered and stigmatized, depending on the cultural context and prevailing social norms. Some examples of tattoo stigma across cultures and time periods include:

- Ancient Rome and Greece: While tattoos were occasionally used as symbols of status or religious devotion, they were also employed as a means of marking slaves and criminals, leading to a negative association with tattoos in these societies.
- Japan: Although tattooing has a long history in Japan, tattoos have been stigmatized due to their association with the Yakuza, the Japanese organized crime syndicate. As a result, tattoos are often viewed with suspicion and are sometimes even banned in public spaces, such as hot springs and swimming pools.
- Western societies: In the early 20th century, tattoos were often associated with sailors, soldiers, and working-class individuals, leading to a perception of tattoos as low-class or deviant. However, this perception has shifted significantly in recent years, as tattoos have become more mainstream and accepted.

Tattoos and the Law

Legal restrictions surrounding tattoos vary widely across different jurisdictions and can have a significant impact on the social perception of tattoos. Some examples include:

- Age restrictions: Many countries and states enforce minimum age requirements for obtaining a tattoo, typically ranging from 16 to 18 years old. This legislation is intended to protect minors from making impulsive decisions that could have long-lasting consequences.
- Licensing and regulation: Tattoo artists and studios are often subject to strict licensing and regulatory requirements, including sanitation standards and the use of approved inks and equipment.
- Tattooing in prisons: In many countries, tattooing is illegal within prisons due to concerns about the spread of infectious diseases and the use of tattoos as gang identifiers. Despite these restrictions, underground tattooing remains prevalent in prison settings, often using improvised equipment and inks.

Tattoos in the Workplace and Professional Settings

The acceptance of tattoos in the workplace and professional settings can vary widely, depending on factors such as industry, company culture, and individual attitudes. While many organizations have become more accepting of tattoos, some professions and companies may still enforce strict dress codes or policies regarding visible tattoos. These restrictions can sometimes lead to discrimination or unequal treatment for tattooed individuals in the workforce.

The Evolving Social Acceptance of Tattoos

As tattoos have become increasingly popular and mainstream, the social stigma surrounding them has begun to fade in many cultures. Factors contributing to the growing acceptance of tattoos include:

- The influence of popular culture: Celebrities, athletes, and other public figures who display tattoos can help to normalize and destigmatize tattoos in the public eye.
- Greater visibility: As more people from diverse backgrounds and professions choose to get tattooed, the perception of tattoos as exclusively associated with certain subcultures or social classes has diminished.
- Artistic evolution: The increasing sophistication and creativity of tattoo art has helped to elevate the perception of tattoos as a legitimate form of artistic expression.

In this chapter, we have explored the complex web of taboos and social perceptions surrounding tattoos, examining how cultural factors, legal restrictions, and workplace policies have shaped attitudes towards tattoo art and culture. As social acceptance of tattoos continues to grow and evolve, it is important to recognize and challenge the lingering prejudices and stigmas that may still exist in some settings. By fostering open dialogue and understanding about the diverse meanings and motivations behind tattoos, we can work towards a more inclusive and accepting society where individuals are free to express themselves through the art of ink without fear of judgment or discrimination.

The journey towards greater acceptance of tattoos is an ongoing process, and while significant progress has been made, there is still work to be done. As we continue to embrace the rich history, symbolism, and artistic potential of tattoos, we can help to challenge misconceptions and dismantle the remaining barriers that stand in the way of a truly inclusive tattoo culture. By doing so, we not only empower individuals to express their unique identities and stories through tattoo art, but also pave the way for future generations to explore and celebrate the transformative power of ink.

THE FUTURE OF TATTOOS

I n this chapter, we will delve into the exciting possibilities for the future of tattoos, exploring how technological advancements and cultural shifts are shaping the world of tattooing. From electronic tattoos to biotech ink, the boundaries of what is possible in tattoo art are constantly being pushed, reflecting the ever-changing role of tattoos in personal expression and identity.

Technological Advancements in Tattooing

As technology continues to evolve, so too do the possibilities for tattoo art. Some cutting-edge developments in the world of tattoos include:

- Electronic tattoos: Also known as e-tattoos or smart tattoos, these innovative designs incorporate electronic components and sensors into flexible, wearable devices that adhere to the skin. Electronic tattoos have the potential to monitor vital signs, track physical activity, or even interface with other electronic devices, offering a fusion of art and technology that is both functional and visually striking.

- Biotech tattoos: Biotech tattoos utilize specially engineered ink to create designs that interact with the wearer's body or environment. Examples include color-changing ink that reacts to temperature or UV light, and ink that contains live, genetically modified microorganisms that can respond to various stimuli, such as changes in blood sugar levels or exposure to certain chemicals.

- 3D-printed tattoos: As 3D printing technology advances, tattoo artists are exploring its potential for creating intricate, detailed designs. 3D-printed tattoos can be crafted using a variety of materials, from traditional tattoo ink to biocompatible polymers, allowing for unprecedented levels of customization and complexity in tattoo art.

The Ongoing Evolution of Tattoo Art and Culture

As tattoo art and culture continue to evolve, we can expect to see new styles, techniques, and trends emerging in response to shifting societal values and artistic influences. Some possible directions for the future of tattoo art include:

- Fusion of traditional and modern styles: As the tattoo community becomes more globalized, artists from diverse cultural backgrounds are increasingly collaborating and sharing techniques, resulting in innovative designs that blend traditional motifs with contemporary aesthetics.
- Expanded use of color and materials: Advancements in tattoo ink technology are allowing for a greater range of vibrant, long-lasting colors, as well as the development of alternative materials, such as metallic or glow-in-the-dark inks, that offer new possibilities for creative expression.
- Emphasis on personalization and storytelling: As tattoos become increasingly mainstream, individuals are seeking designs that reflect their unique personalities and life experiences, leading to a growing emphasis on custom, one-of-a-kind tattoos that tell a personal story.

The Role of Tattoos in Personal Expression and Identity

Tattoos have long served as a powerful medium for self-expression and identity, and this is likely to continue into the future. As societal attitudes towards tattoos become more accepting, and as new technologies and artistic styles emerge, tattoos will continue to offer individuals a means to:

- Celebrate their heritage and cultural roots: Tattoo designs that draw on traditional motifs or cultural symbols can help individuals connect with their ancestral heritage and express pride in their cultural identity.
- Commemorate significant life events: Tattoos can serve as a lasting reminder of important milestones, such as overcoming adversity, celebrating achievements, or honoring the memory of a loved one.
- Reflect personal beliefs and values: Tattoos can be a powerful way to express an individual's beliefs, values, or spiritual convictions, whether through religious symbols, philosophical quotes, or designs that represent a personal ethos.

In this chapter, we have explored the exciting possibilities for the future of tattoos, examining how technological advancements and cultural shifts are shaping the world of tattoo art and its role in personal expression and identity. As we look forward to the continued evolution of tattoos, we can appreciate the myriad ways in which they offer a canvas for creativity, self-expression, and connection. From cutting-edge electronic tattoos to deeply personal designs that tell a unique story, the future of tattoo art is bound to be as diverse and dynamic as the individuals who wear them.

TATTOO AFTERCARE AND REMOVAL

In this final chapter, we will discuss the essential aspects of tattoo aftercare and the various methods of tattoo removal. As tattoos become an increasingly popular form of self-expression, it is important to understand the proper care and maintenance required to preserve their appearance and ensure their longevity. Additionally, we will examine the reasons people may choose to remove their tattoos and the available techniques for doing so.

Tattoo Aftercare

Proper aftercare is crucial for the healing and preservation of a new tattoo. Following a tattoo artist's aftercare instructions can help prevent infection, minimize scarring, and ensure that the tattoo remains vibrant and sharp. While specific recommendations may vary, some general guidelines for tattoo aftercare include:

- Keep the tattoo clean and dry: Gently wash the tattoo with mild, unscented soap and water, and avoid submerging it in water for extended periods.
- Moisturize the tattoo: Apply a thin layer of unscented, alcohol-free lotion or ointment to the tattoo several times a day, as directed by the tattoo artist.
- Avoid sun exposure: Keep the tattoo out of direct sunlight, and apply a high-SPF sunscreen once the tattoo has fully healed to prevent fading and sun damage.
- Allow the tattoo to breathe: Avoid covering the tattoo with tight, restrictive clothing, and refrain from using plastic wrap or bandages, except as instructed by the tattoo artist.
- Resist the urge to scratch or pick: As the tattoo heals, it may become itchy or form scabs. Avoid scratching or picking at the tattoo, as this can damage the ink and cause scarring.

Tattoo Removal

There are various reasons why someone might choose to remove a tattoo, such as regret, changing personal tastes, or the desire to make a fresh start. Fortunately, there are several methods available for tattoo removal, ranging from traditional techniques to cutting-edge laser technology.

- Laser tattoo removal: This is the most popular and effective method of tattoo removal. Using specialized lasers, the ink particles in the skin are broken down and absorbed by the body's immune system. Multiple sessions are often required, and the process can be painful and expensive.
- Dermabrasion: This method involves the removal of the outer layers of skin using an abrasive tool, effectively "sanding" away the tattoo. Dermabrasion can be painful and carries the risk of scarring and pigmentation changes.
- Surgical excision: In this method, a surgeon removes the tattooed skin and sutures the remaining skin together. This technique is generally reserved for smaller tattoos and carries the risk of scarring.
- TCA (Trichloroacetic Acid) peels: This involves the application of a chemical solution to the skin, causing it to peel away and reveal the underlying layers. TCA peels can be effective for some tattoos but may

require multiple sessions and carry the risk of scarring and pigmentation changes.

- Tattoo removal creams: Some over-the-counter creams claim to remove tattoos by breaking down the ink particles in the skin. However, these creams are often ineffective and may cause skin irritation or damage.

We have journeyed through the fascinating history, cultural significance, and artistic evolution of tattoos. From ancient tribal markings to modern masterpieces, tattoos have long served as powerful symbols of identity, faith, and creativity. As we look to the future of tattoo art and technology, we can appreciate the diverse ways in which tattoos continue to shape and reflect our personal and collective stories.

APPENDIX A: A COMPREHENSIVE GUIDE TO TATTOO STYLES

In this appendix, we will provide a detailed breakdown of several popular tattoo styles, delving into their history, characteristics, and visual examples. This guide will help readers familiarize themselves with the diverse range of tattoo styles that have developed across different cultures and time periods.

American Traditional

Also known as "Old School" or "Sailor Jerry" style, American Traditional tattoos are characterized by bold black outlines, a limited color palette (primarily red, green, yellow, and black), and iconic designs such as anchors, roses, skulls, and eagles. This style originated among sailors in the early 20th century and gained widespread popularity in the United

States through the work of artists like Norman "Sailor Jerry" Collins and Ed Hardy.

Neo-Traditional

Neo-Traditional tattoos build upon the foundations of American Traditional style, incorporating more detailed designs, a wider color palette, and a greater emphasis on realism. While Neo-Traditional tattoos often feature similar subject matter as American Traditional designs, they frequently include modern elements, such as pop culture references and surrealistic imagery. This style gained popularity in the late 20th and early 21st centuries and continues to evolve today.

Japanese

Japanese tattoos, also known as "Irezumi" or "Horimono," have a long and storied history dating back centuries. This style is characterized by intricate designs featuring mythical creatures, animals, and nature motifs, often rendered in a highly detailed, full-body format. Common themes in Japanese tattoos include dragons, koi fish, cherry blossoms, and samurai warriors. This style has influenced many Western tattoo artists and is celebrated for its bold, intricate designs and cultural symbolism.

Blackwork

Blackwork tattoos utilize heavy, bold black ink to create striking designs that often incorporate geometric shapes, patterns, and intricate linework. This style has roots in tribal tattooing traditions and is influenced by a variety of cultures, from Polynesian to Celtic. Blackwork designs can range from simple, minimalist symbols to elaborate, full-body pieces and are prized for their strong visual impact.

Dotwork

Dotwork tattoos are created by using individual dots of ink to form intricate designs, patterns, and shading. This style is often used in conjunction with geometric or mandala designs and can also be employed to create stunning, realistic portraits and images. Dotwork tattoos are known for their delicate, detailed appearance and the patience and skill required of the artist to execute them.

Watercolor

Watercolor tattoos emulate the fluid, painterly aesthetic of watercolor paintings, incorporating soft, translucent colors and blending techniques to create a dreamy, ethereal effect. This style often features loose, flowing lines and abstract or impressionistic designs. While watercolor tattoos have gained popularity in recent years, some concerns have been raised about the potential for the colors to fade or blur over time, making proper aftercare and maintenance especially important for this style.

These are just a few of the many diverse tattoo styles that have emerged over the years. As tattoo art and culture continue to evolve, new styles and techniques are constantly being developed, offering endless possibilities for self-expression and creativity in the world of ink.

APPENDIX B: NOTABLE TATTOO ARTISTS AND PIONEERS

In this appendix, we will profile several influential tattoo artists and pioneers who have left a lasting impact on tattoo culture and contributed to the development and evolution of the art form across various styles and periods.

Samuel O'Reilly (1854-1908)

Samuel O'Reilly, an Irish-American tattoo artist, is credited with inventing the first electric tattoo machine in 1891, which revolutionized the tattooing process by allowing for faster and more precise application of ink. O'Reilly's invention laid the foundation for modern tattoo machines and had a profound influence on the industry.

Norman "Sailor Jerry" Collins (1911-1973)

Norman "Sailor Jerry" Collins was an American tattoo artist who rose to prominence in the mid-20th century. He is best known for his iconic American Traditional tattoo designs, which featured bold lines, vivid colors, and timeless imagery such as skulls, roses, and eagles. Sailor Jerry's innovative techniques and distinctive artistic style continue to inspire tattoo artists today.

Horiyoshi III (b. 1946)

Horiyoshi III, born Yoshihito Nakano, is a renowned Japanese tattoo artist who has dedicated his life to mastering the traditional art of Irezumi. He is known for his intricate, full-body tattoos featuring mythological creatures, nature motifs, and scenes from Japanese folklore. Horiyoshi III's work has helped to preserve and promote the rich cultural heritage of Japanese tattooing, and he has trained many notable apprentices who continue to carry on the tradition.

Don Ed Hardy (b. 1945)

Don Ed Hardy is an American tattoo artist who has been credited with popularizing tattoo culture in the mainstream through his unique fusion of American Traditional and Japanese tattoo styles. Hardy's detailed, colorful designs and innovative techniques have inspired countless artists and collectors. In addition to his work as a tattoo artist, Hardy has also enjoyed success in the world of fashion with his eponymous clothing line, which features his signature tattoo designs.

Kat Von D (b. 1982)

Born Katherine von Drachenberg, Kat Von D is a Mexican-American tattoo artist, television personality, and entrepreneur. She gained widespread recognition as a star of the reality TV show "LA Ink," which showcased her unique artistic style and impressive skill. Kat Von D has since gone on to open her own tattoo studio, High Voltage Tattoo, and launch a successful cosmetics line.

Filip Leu (b. 1967)

Filip Leu is a Swiss tattoo artist known for his groundbreaking work in the realms of biomechanical and surrealistic tattoo art. As a member of the renowned Leu Family, Filip has been immersed in the world of tattooing from a young age and has developed a distinct, avant-garde style that has inspired countless artists around the world.

Ami James (b. 1972)

Ami James is an Israeli-American tattoo artist, television personality, and entrepreneur who rose to fame as the co-owner of the Love Hate Tattoo Studio in Miami, Florida, and star of the reality TV show "Miami Ink." James has been influential in popularizing tattoo culture on a global scale and has since gone on to open additional tattoo studios and launch various ventures in the tattoo industry.

These notable tattoo artists and pioneers have each made significant contributions to the world of tattoo art and culture, shaping the industry's evolution and inspiring future generations of artists and enthusiasts. Their impact is felt not only in the designs they created but also in the countless lives they've touched through their artistic expression and dedication to the craft.

APPENDIX C: TATTOO CONVENTIONS AND EVENTS

In this appendix, we will provide a list of popular tattoo conventions and events from around the world. These gatherings serve as a platform for tattoo artists and enthusiasts to connect, share ideas, showcase their work, and celebrate the diverse world of tattoo art and culture. Please note that the dates provided may change yearly, so it's essential to check the respective event websites for the most up-to-date information.

London Tattoo Convention (United Kingdom)

Held annually in late September, the London Tattoo Convention brings together over 400 of the world's best tattoo artists, showcasing their work and offering live tattooing sessions. The event also features live music, art exhibitions, tattoo competitions, and seminars.

Mondial du Tatouage (Paris Tattoo Convention) (France)

One of the most prestigious tattoo conventions globally, Mondial du Tatouage takes place in Paris annually, usually in February or March. This event attracts renowned tattoo artists and thousands of visitors, offering live tattooing, art exhibitions, tattoo contests, and live performances.

International Brussels Tattoo Convention (Belgium)

The International Brussels Tattoo Convention is held annually in November, featuring top tattoo artists from around the globe, live tattooing, body modification shows, art exhibitions, and live entertainment.

The NY Empire State Tattoo Expo (United States)

Held in New York City, typically in July, the NY Empire State Tattoo Expo gathers top tattoo artists from around the world, providing live tattooing, art exhibitions, tattoo contests, and seminars. The event showcases a wide variety of styles and techniques, making it a must-attend for tattoo enthusiasts.

Sydney Tattoo & Body Art Expo (Australia)

Taking place annually in March, the Sydney Tattoo & Body Art Expo is one of the largest tattoo events in the Southern Hemisphere, featuring live tattooing by renowned artists, tattoo competitions, art exhibitions, and live entertainment.

Ink Mania Expo (Netherlands)

Ink Mania Expo is an annual tattoo convention held in June, attracting top tattoo artists from around the world. The event offers live tattooing, workshops, seminars, tattoo contests, and a variety of entertainment options, including live music and performances.

The Biggest Tattoo Show on Earth (United States)

Held in Las Vegas, The Biggest Tattoo Show on Earth lives up to its name as one of the largest tattoo conventions globally. The event, typically taking place in October, features live tattooing by hundreds of artists, seminars, tattoo competitions, and a wide range of entertainment options.

Milano Tattoo Convention (Italy)

The Milano Tattoo Convention, held annually in February, is one of the most prestigious tattoo events in Europe. The event showcases the work of hundreds of international tattoo artists and features live tattooing, tattoo contests, art exhibitions, and live performances.

These are just a few of the many tattoo conventions and events that take place worldwide, celebrating the art and culture of tattooing. By attending these gatherings, artists and enthusiasts can connect, learn from one another, and share their passion for this unique and diverse form of artistic expression.

APPENDIX D: TATTOO TERMINOLOGY GLOSSARY

Here's a comprehensive glossary of common tattoo-related terms, phrases, and jargon to help readers familiarize themselves with the language of tattoo art and culture.

Aftercare: The process of caring for a new tattoo to promote proper healing and prevent infection or other complications.

Autoclave: A machine used to sterilize tattoo equipment, such as needles and tubes, by subjecting them to high-pressure steam at a specific temperature.

Black and grey: A tattoo style that uses only black ink, with varying shades of grey achieved through dilution and shading techniques.

Blackwork: A tattoo style characterized by the use of bold, black ink to create striking designs, often incorporating geometric shapes, patterns, and intricate linework.

Blowout: A tattoo imperfection that occurs when ink is applied too deeply, causing it to spread out under the skin and create a blurred effect.

Body suit: A full-body tattoo, often composed of multiple interconnected designs or a single, large-scale design.

Flash: Pre-drawn tattoo designs, typically displayed on the walls of a tattoo studio for clients to choose from.

Freehand: A tattooing technique in which the artist draws the design directly onto the skin, without using a stencil.

Irezumi: Traditional Japanese tattooing, characterized by intricate, full-body designs featuring mythological creatures, nature motifs, and scenes from Japanese folklore.

Linework: The outline or basic structure of a tattoo design, usually created using a single needle or a small group of needles.

Machine (also known as Tattoo Gun): The tool used by tattoo artists to apply ink to the skin, typically composed of a needle, tube, and motor.

Neo-Traditional: A tattoo style that builds upon the foundations of American Traditional, incorporating more detailed designs, a wider color palette, and a greater emphasis on realism.

Rotary machine: A type of tattoo machine that uses an electric motor to move the needle up and down, offering a smoother and quieter operation compared to coil machines.

Stencil: A transferable outline of a tattoo design, created on specialized paper and applied to the skin to serve as a guide for the tattoo artist.

Stick and poke: A tattooing technique that involves manually inserting ink into the skin using a needle, without the use of a tattoo machine. Also known as "hand-poked" tattoos.

Tattoo cover-up: A tattoo design created specifically to conceal or mask an existing tattoo, typically using more substantial imagery, shading, or colors.

Tattoo fade: The gradual lightening or blurring of a tattoo's colors and lines over time, often due to sun exposure, poor aftercare, or the natural aging process.

Tattoo session: The period during which a tattoo artist works on a client's tattoo, typically lasting several hours.

Touch-up: The process of adding or correcting small details in a healed tattoo, often performed to address any fading, imperfections, or changes in the design.

Watercolor: A tattoo style that emulates the fluid, painterly aesthetic of watercolor paintings, incorporating soft, translucent colors and blending techniques.

This glossary covers some of the most common tattoo-related terms and phrases, providing readers with a basic understanding of the language and terminology used within the tattoo art and culture.

APPENDIX E: HOW TO CHOOSE THE RIGHT TATTOO DESIGN AND PLACEMENT

Choosing the perfect tattoo design and placement can be a daunting task, as it's a lifelong commitment that reflects your personal style, values, and experiences. This appendix will provide tips and considerations to help guide you through the process and make an informed decision.

Personal style and meaning

Consider your personal style and what resonates with you when selecting a tattoo design. It could be something that holds personal significance, such as a symbol of your heritage, a favorite quote, or an image that represents a pivotal life experience. Remember that your tattoo will be a part of you for the rest of your life, so choose something that you feel connected to and proud to display.

Cultural significance and sensitivity

If you're considering a tattoo design inspired by a particular culture or tradition, it's essential to research its origins, meaning, and cultural significance. Be respectful and mindful of cultural appropriation; some symbols and designs hold deep cultural or religious meaning and may not be appropriate for those outside of that community. Always strive to be respectful and informed about the cultural context of the design you choose.

Size and complexity

The size and complexity of your desired tattoo design will play a role in its placement and overall impact. Smaller, simpler designs are often more versatile and can be easily placed on various areas of the body. Larger, more intricate designs may require more space, limiting placement options. Consider whether you want a single, standalone design or something that can be easily incorporated into a larger piece in the future.

Tattoo visibility

When choosing the placement of your tattoo, think about how visible you want it to be. Some people prefer tattoos that are easily hidden for professional or personal reasons, while others opt for more visible designs as a bold statement. If you're concerned about potential job restrictions or the opinions of friends and family members, consider opting for a more discreet location, such as the upper arm, thigh, or back.

Pain tolerance

Different areas of the body have varying pain levels during the tattooing process. Areas with thin skin or close proximity to bones, such as the ribs, ankles, and fingers, tend to be more painful. If you have a low pain tolerance or are getting your first tattoo, consider choosing a less sensitive area like the outer arm, shoulder, or calf.

Consult with a professional

Once you have a general idea of the design and placement you want, consult with a professional tattoo artist. They can help you refine your ideas, provide input on the design's feasibility, and suggest any necessary modifications. Tattoo artists have extensive knowledge of their craft and can offer invaluable advice on selecting the perfect design and placement for your body.

By considering these factors and consulting with a professional, you'll be better equipped to choose the perfect tattoo design and placement that suits your personal style, values, and lifestyle. Remember, a tattoo is a lifelong commitment, so take your time and ensure that you're making the best decision for yourself.

ABOUT THE AUTHOR

Rhyan Scorpio-Rhys is a tattoo aficionado and scholar of the arcane arts, deeply immersed in the rich history of tattoo culture and supernatural lore. With an insatiable curiosity for the mystical and the esoteric, Rhyan has traveled the globe in search of the world's most enigmatic tattoo masters and their cryptic practices.

Born to a family of tattoo artists and historians, Rhyan developed an early appreciation for the traditional craft and the symbols that permeate the diverse world of tattoo art. His studies led him to the ancient wisdom of various cultures, unearthing secrets long-hidden within the intricate lines and sacred patterns of the tattoos adorning the skin of their bearers.

A master storyteller, Rhyan weaves together fact and myth, unraveling the legends surrounding the supernatural aspects of tattooing. He has dedicated his life to chronicling the timeless stories that shed light on the connection between the spiritual realm and the art etched onto the skin. Rhyan's vast knowledge of ancient civilizations, occult practices, and forgotten rituals imbue his writing with an otherworldly aura, captivating readers and drawing them into the mysterious world of tattoo lore.

As a prominent figure within the tattoo community, Rhyan is highly regarded for his unique ability to transcend time and space, unearthing the stories that bind humanity across generations and cultures. His enigmatic presence, coupled with his deep understanding of the unseen forces that govern the world of tattoos, has made him a highly sought-after speaker at conventions and seminars around the world.

Through his writing, Rhyan Scorpio-Rhys invites readers to embark on a journey of discovery, exploring the enigmatic world of tattoos and the supernatural forces that shape our existence. Be prepared to enter a realm of wonder, where ancient symbols hold the key to unlocking the secrets of our past and charting the course of our collective future.

www.ingramcontent.com/pod-product-compliance
Lightning Source LLC
Chambersburg PA
CBHW071032220526
45467CB00004B/1626